# *Just* COOKIES
## COOKBOOK

### HOLIDAY RECIPES

Cathy Marie Hake and Deborah Boone

BARBOUR
PUBLISHING

© 2003 by Barbour Publishing, Inc.

ISBN 978-1-59789-800-3

ll rights reserved. No part of this publication may be reproduced or transmitted for commercial purposes, except for brief quotations in printed reviews, without written permission of the publisher.

Churches and noncommercial interests may reproduce portions of this book without the express written permission of Barbour Publishing, provided that the text does not exceed 500 words and that the text is not material quoted from another publisher. When reproducing text from this book, include the following credit line: "From *Just Cookies Cookbook: Holiday Recipes and More*, published by Barbour Publishing, Inc. Used by permission."

All scripture quotations, unless otherwise indicated, are taken from the HOLY BIBLE, NEW INTERNATIONAL VERSION®. NIV®. Copyright © 1973, 1978, 1984 by International Bible Society. Used by permission of Zondervan. All rights reserved.

Scripture quotations marked KJV are taken from the King James Version of the Bible.

Published by Barbour Publishing, Inc., P.O. Box 719, Uhrichsville, Ohio 44683, www.barbourbooks.com

*Our mission is to publish and distribute inspirational products offering exceptional value and biblical encouragement to the masses.*

Printed in Canada.

# Contents

Nothing warms a home like a fire on the hearth and fresh cookies in the oven. Light those logs, then tie on your apron. With this simple collection of recipes, you'll find everything you need—from the easy to make-aheads, family favorites, and scrumptious festive cookies for entertaining.

Decorate some to create a pretty platter for a buffet table, make some for gifts, or let the kids get involved. Whatever appeals to you, don't miss out on a traditional and fun way to celebrate the Christmas holiday!

For unto us a child is born, unto us a son is given: and the government shall be upon his shoulder: and his name shall be called Wonderful, Counsellor, The mighty God, The everlasting Father, The Prince of Peace.

ISAIAH 9:6 KJV

# Christmas Joy Cookies

1 cup of warm memories                    1 cup of devotion
1 cup of consideration for others    2 cups of laughter
2 cups of gratitude                          3 cups of love

Mix thoroughly.
Flavor with hugs and kisses.
Blend well and fold into daily life.
Bake well with the warmth of human kindness and serve with a smile.

# Holiday Festives

True happiness comes from the joy of deeds
well done, the zest of creating things new.

ANTOINE DE SAINT-EXUPERY

*Write blessings and Bible verses on strips of paper before mixing the recipe that follows.*

Here are some suggestions for "blessings." Feel free to get creative.

Peace on earth will come to stay,
When we live Christmas every day.
HELEN STEINER RICE

A friend is a blessing you give yourself.

Good friends make the holidays happy.

The good you do today may quickly be forgotten,
but the impact of what you do will never disappear.

The safest place to be is within the will of God.

"The good man brings good things out of the
good stored up in his heart."
LUKE 6:45

A candle loses nothing by lighting another candle.
ERIN MAJORS

I asked God for all things that I might enjoy life.
He gave me life that I might enjoy all things.
GEN. JOHN P. JUMPER

The cheerful heart has a continual feast.
PROVERBS 15:15

As honey is sweet and pleasant to the taste, so wisdom is to the soul.
SEE PROVERBS 24:13–14

# Christmas Blessing Cookies

These cookies can be packed in Chinese takeout containers and given as a gift.

| | |
|---|---|
| ½ cup cake flour | 4 tablespoons cooking oil |
| 2 tablespoons cornstarch | 2 egg whites |
| 4 tablespoons sugar | 2 tablespoons water |
| Dash salt | 2 drops red food coloring |

Sift together the dry ingredients and add salt. Add oil and egg whites; stir until smooth. Add water and food coloring; mix well. Make one cookie at a time by pouring 1 tablespoon batter onto lightly greased skillet. Spread to 3½-inch circle. Cook over low heat for 4 minutes or until lightly browned. Flip with spatula and cook 1 more minute. Slide out onto pot holder and work swiftly: Put blessing in center, fold cookie in half, then bend in half over edge of a bowl. Place in a muffin pan to cool.

# Pfeffernusse

3 eggs
½ pound powdered sugar
1 lemon, juice and rind
2 cups flour
¼ teaspoon salt

½ teaspoon baking soda
¼ teaspoon cloves
½ teaspoon cinnamon
¼ teaspoon nutmeg

Beat eggs well. Gradually add powdered sugar, lemon juice, and grated rind. Sift flour, salt, soda, and spices. Sift a second time. Add to egg mixture. Beat to form smooth, medium-soft dough. Chill in refrigerator for several hours. Roll out on floured board into long finger-shaped sticks. Cut into marble-sized pieces. Bake at 425 degrees on greased cookie sheet until light golden brown.

# Berlinerkranzer

*These little Norwegian wreath cookies are a traditional favorite.*

**Dough:**

| | |
|---|---|
| ¾ cup butter, softened | 2 teaspoons grated orange peel |
| ¼ cup shortening | 2 eggs |
| 1 cup sugar | 4 cups flour |

Cream butter, shortening, and sugar. Add orange peel and eggs. Mix in flour. Roll dough by rounded teaspoonfuls into ropes about 6 inches long. Form each rope into a circle, bringing one end over and through into a single knot (kind of like a shoelace). Let ends extend ½ inch. Place on ungreased cookie sheet.

**Glaze and decoration:**

| | |
|---|---|
| 1 egg white | Red candied cherries |
| 2 tablespoons sugar | Green candied citron |

Beat egg white until foamy, adding sugar 1 tablespoon at a time. Brush tops of cookies with egg white mixture. Press tiny bits of candied cherries on center of knot for holly berries, and make little leaves from the candied citron. Bake at 400 degrees for 10–12 minutes or until set. Do not let brown. Immediately remove from baking sheet.

# Red Ribbons

*Red ribbons add color and beauty to a cookie assortment.*

1 cup butter, softened
2 ½ cups all-purpose flour
½ cup sugar
1 egg, slightly beaten
1 teaspoon vanilla

¼ teaspoon salt
Strawberry jam or raspberry jelly
Water
¾ cup confectioners' sugar

Beat the butter with an electric mixer on medium to high speed for 30 seconds. Add about half of the flour, then the sugar, egg, vanilla, and salt. Beat until thoroughly mixed. Add in the remaining flour, mixing until the dough sticks together to form a ball. Lightly knead ball. Divide the cookie dough into 8 equal portions. On a lightly floured surface, roll each portion of dough into a 9-inch rope. Place the ropes on an ungreased cookie sheet about 2 inches apart. Press a groove down the length of each rope with the handle of a wooden spoon. Bake in a 375-degree oven for 10 minutes. Spoon jam or jelly into groove and bake until edges begin to brown slightly (about 5 minutes). Cool on cookie sheet for 5 minutes. Using a large spatula, remove cookies to a cutting board. Mix water and confectioners' sugar to form a glaze. Drizzle over hot cookies. Cut into 1-inch slices. Move cookies to wire rack to finish cooling.

# Cinnamon Twisties

2 cups sugar
2 cups ground walnuts
1 tablespoon cinnamon
½ pound butter

½ pound cream cheese
2½ cups flour
1 egg, beaten

Mix together sugar, walnuts, and cinnamon and set aside. In another bowl, cream butter and cream cheese together. Gradually add flour. If dough is too soft, add a little more flour. Roll out dough to ½-inch thick and brush with beaten egg. Cover with cinnamon mixture. Cut into 1½-inch strips and twist. Place on cookie sheet. Bake at 400 degrees for 8–10 minutes.

# Grandma Ruth's Finger Cookies

(From the kitchen of Ruth Hermestroff)
*These treats are also known as wedding cakes and crescents.*

1 cup butter
1 cup flour
1 teaspoon vanilla

1 cup finely chopped pecans
1 teaspoon water
3 tablespoons powdered sugar

Mix all ingredients well and chill for at least an hour. Roll in palm of hand and shape into crescents or roll into balls. Bake at 375 degrees for 10 minutes. Cool and roll in powdered sugar.

# Chocolate-Striped Cookies

½ cup butter
½ cup shortening
1 cup sugar
½ teaspoon baking soda
⅛ teaspoon salt
1 egg
2 tablespoons milk
1 teaspoon vanilla

3 cups all-purpose flour
⅓ cup semisweet chocolate pieces,
   melted and cooled
½ cup finely chopped nuts
½ cup miniature semisweet
   chocolate pieces
¼ teaspoon almond extract

Beat butter and shortening on medium to high speed for 30 seconds. Add sugar, baking soda, and salt; beat until combined. Beat in the egg, milk, and vanilla. Beat in as much of the flour as you can with the mixer, then stir in remaining flour by hand. Divide dough in half. Knead the melted chocolate and nuts into half of the dough. Knead the miniature chocolate pieces and almond extract into the other half of dough. Divide each portion of dough in half. Line the bottom and sides of a 9x5x3-inch loaf pan with plastic wrap. Press half of the chocolate dough evenly in pan. Layer in the vanilla, the remaining chocolate, then the last vanilla to form four even, flat layers. Invert pan to remove dough and peel off plastic wrap. Cut dough crosswise into $1/4$-inch-thick slices. Place cookies 2 inches apart on an ungreased cookie sheet. Bake cookies in a 375-degree oven for about 10 minutes.

Tip: *This dough can be made and frozen in a plastic freezer bag up to a month in advance.*

# Pecan Dainties

*These delightful cookies are reminiscent of pecan pie.*

**Cheese Pastry:**

1 3-ounce package cream cheese      1 cup sifted flour
½ cup butter

Blend cream cheese and butter. Stir in flour. Chill one hour. Shape into 2 dozen 1-inch balls. Place in ungreased muffin tin and thumbprint the dough to create indentation for filling.

**Pecan Filling:**

1 egg

1 tablespoon butter

Dash of salt

¾ cup brown sugar

1 teaspoon vanilla

⅔ cup chopped pecans

Beat all ingredients (except pecans) until smooth. Divide ½ of pecans among pastry. Top with mixture. Top with remaining pecans. Bake at 350 degrees for 25 minutes.

Tip: *The easiest way to keep these cookies uniform is to use a 1¾-inch muffin tin, but they can be made on a regular cookie sheet.*

# Snowman Butter Cookies

1 cup butter softened
   (margarine doesn't work as well)
$\frac{1}{2}$ cup sugar
$\frac{1}{4}$ teaspoon almond extract

$2\frac{1}{2}$ cups all-purpose flour
1 teaspoon water
Red and green food coloring
Black and orange jimmies or sprinkles

Cream butter, sugar, and extract. Gradually beat in flour and water. Remove $\frac{1}{3}$ cup of mix into small bowls and tint red. Do the same with green; set aside. Shape remaining dough into 12 1-inch balls and 12 1$\frac{1}{2}$-inch balls. Place one smaller ball above one larger ball on ungreased baking sheet; flatten slightly. Use 2 teaspoons of colored dough and form into a hat (make 6 of each color). Place above head. Form scarf from $\frac{1}{4}$ teaspoon of each color into a 3-inch rope. Twist ropes together, leaving one end a little "unraveled." Place scarf around snowman's neck. Insert jimmies for eyes and nose. Bake at 350 degrees for 15–18 minutes or until set. Cool on baking sheets.

# Sandbakkels

1 cup butter
1 cup sugar
1 egg, slightly beaten

3 cups flour
1 teaspoon vanilla or almond
    flavoring

Cream together the butter and sugar. Add egg, flour, and vanilla or almond flavoring. Mix well. Chill about 2 hours. Press into metal molds. Bake at 350 degrees for 5–6 minutes, until light brown.

Tip: *These cookies are baked in fluted metal molds, which can be purchased at Scandinavian shops or specialty cooking shops.*

# Krumkake

*Krumkake may be eaten plain or filled with
sweetened whipped cream and strawberries.*

½ cup whipping cream
3 eggs
1 cup sugar
1¼ cups flour

½ cup melted butter
1 teaspoon ground
    cardamom or almond extract

Whip the cream. Beat eggs lightly and add to the cream. Add remaining ingredients. Bake on a krumkake iron. Turn the iron once while baking each cookie. Remove krumkake from the iron with a spatula. Roll at once around a wooden krumkake roller; cool and remove.

Tip: *These thin, cone-shaped cookies are made on a special decorative iron. Most waffle irons have reversible plates with this decoration on the reverse side.*

# Swedish Pepparkakor

(From the kitchen of Tracie Peterson)
*Swedish pepparkakor are also known as gingersnaps.*

| | |
|---|---|
| 1 cup butter (not margarine) | 1 teaspoon baking soda |
| 1½ cups sugar | 1 teaspoon ginger |
| 1 egg | 1 teaspoon cloves |
| 1 tablespoon dark syrup | 2 teaspoons cinnamon |
| 3 cups flour, sifted | |

Cream the butter, sugar, egg, and syrup. Sift in the flour, baking soda, and the spices. Cover and chill for at least 2 hours. Roll out and cut with cookie cutter. Bake at 375 degrees for 10 minutes.

# Butterhorn Cookies

(From the kitchen of Luisa Stoner)

2 cubes butter
2 ½ cups flour

1 egg yolk
¾ cup sour cream

**Cinnamon Mix:**
¾ cup sugar
1 teaspoon cinnamon

¾ cup chopped almonds

Work butter into flour with fingers. Add egg yolk and sour cream, blending well. Shape into ball, sprinkle with flour, and wrap with waxed paper. Chill for several hours or days (the longer the better). Divide chilled dough into 4 pieces and roll one at a time with rolling pin into a circle as if making a piecrust. Roll out to ⅛-inch thickness. Sprinkle with cinnamon mixture and cut into pieces as if cutting a pie. (Be sure to use lots of cinnamon mix.) Roll each piece as if making a crescent roll. Set on greased cookie sheet. Bake at 350 for 20–30 minutes, or until golden brown. Remove quickly from pan and let cool on breadboard or any cold surface.

**Helpful Tip:** *Prepare all your cookies first, before you start baking.*

## Butterscotch Gingerbread Men

½ cup butter, softened
½ cup packed brown sugar
1 small package instant butterscotch
    pudding mix
1 egg

1½ cups flour
1½ teaspoons ground ginger
½ teaspoon baking soda
½ teaspoon ground cinnamon

**Icing:**

2 cups powdered sugar
3 tablespoons milk

Assorted decorator candies
Raisins

Cream butter, brown sugar, and pudding mix. Add egg. Combine flour, ginger, baking soda, and cinnamon; gradually add to the creamed mixture. Cover and refrigerate overnight. On a lightly floured surface, roll out to ⅛-inch thickness. Cut with a 5-inch gingerbread man cutter. Place 1 inch apart on ungreased baking sheets. Bake at 350 degrees for 8–10 minutes or until edges are golden. Remove to wire racks to cool. Combine powdered sugar and milk until smooth. Frost and decorate cookies with candies and raisins.

*"Run, run, run as fast as you can.*
*You can't catch me, I'm the Gingerbread Man!"*

# Candy Cane Twisties

½ cup butter, softened
½ cup shortening
1 cup sugar
¼ cup powdered sugar
½ cup milk
1 egg

1 teaspoon peppermint extract
1 teaspoon vanilla extract
3 ½ cups flour
¼ teaspoon salt
Green and red food coloring

Cream butter, shortening, and sugars. Blend in milk, egg, and extracts. Gradually add flour and salt. Set aside half of dough. Divide remaining dough in half, adding green food coloring to one portion and red to the other. Wrap dough separately in plastic wrap. Refrigerate for 1 hour or until easy to handle. Roll ½ teaspoonfuls of each color of dough into 3-inch ropes. Place each green rope next to a white rope; press together gently and twist. Repeat with red ropes and remaining white ropes. Place 2 inches apart on ungreased baking sheets. Curve one end, forming a cane. Bake at 350 degrees for 11–13 minutes or until set. Cool for 2 minutes; carefully remove to wire racks.

# Ginger Cream Cookies

(From the kitchen of Cindy Malinowski)
*This recipe dates back to the 1880s. For Christmas, decorate them with colored sugars.*

| | |
|---|---|
| ½ cup shortening | 2 teaspoons ground ginger |
| 1 cup sugar | 1 teaspoon ground cloves |
| 2 eggs | 1 teaspoon cinnamon |
| 1 cup molasses | 2 teaspoons baking soda |
| 4 cups flour | 1 cup hot water |
| 1 teaspoon salt | |

Cream the shortening, sugar, and eggs. Add the molasses. Sift dry ingredients together, except for the baking soda. Dissolve the soda in the hot water; then add alternately to the dry ingredients. Chill the dough thoroughly. Drop by teaspoon onto greased cookie sheets 2 inches apart. Bake at 400 degrees for 8 minutes. While still warm, ice with a thin white frosting.

# Grostali

(From the kitchen of Cindy Malinowski)
*This old family recipe comes from Italy.*

| | |
|---|---|
| 6 cups flour, sifted | 1 tablespoon thick cream |
| 1 teaspoon sugar | Grated rind of 1 orange |
| Grated rind of 1 lemon | 2 shots rum |
| 8 eggs | Oil for deep frying |
| 1 teaspoon salt | Powdered sugar |

Mix ingredients; knead good and hard on floured board. Roll very thick and cut in any shape. Fry in deep fat until golden brown. Drain on grocery bags (or some other unglazed paper). Sprinkle with powdered sugar.

# Fattigmands Bakkelser

*A Norwegian holiday favorite!*

10 egg yolks
$1/3$ cup powdered sugar
$1/2$ cup whipping cream
1 tablespoon brandy

1 teaspoon ground cardamom
$1/2$ teaspoon grated lemon peel
2–2 $1/2$ cups flour
Oil for frying

Beat egg yolks and sugar until very thick and lemon-colored (about 10 minutes). Add in cream, brandy, cardamom, and lemon peel. Mix in enough flour until dough is stiff. Chill 3–4 hours. Heat oil to 375 degrees. Divide dough in half. Roll very thin, $1/8$–$1/16$-inch thick. Cut dough into 4x2-inch diamonds. Make a 1-inch slit in center of each. Draw long point of diamond through slit and curl back in opposite direction. Fry in hot fat about 15 seconds on each side, or until light brown. Drain, then sprinkle with powdered sugar. Store in airtight container.

# Torn Pants

(From the kitchen of Shelly Cassara)

4 egg yolks
¼ cup heavy cream
⅓ cup granulated sugar
1 ⅔ cups sifted flour

¼ teaspoon salt
¼ teaspoon cinnamon
Powdered sugar

Beat egg yolks until light. Add cream and sugar; beat well. Add flour, salt, and cinnamon. Chill dough. Divide dough and roll small amount to ⅛-inch thickness. Cut in 1x3-inch strips with pastry wheel, cutting ends diagonally. Make lengthwise slit in center of each strip and pull through. Fry in hot oil (350 degrees) for 2 minutes, or until lightly browned. Drain; sprinkle with powdered sugar.

# Hvite Nötter

*"Little White Mice"*
(This Swedish recipe comes from the kitchen of Tracie Peterson.)

1 cup butter (not margarine)
1/4 cup powdered sugar
1 teaspoon water

1 teaspoon vanilla
2 cups flour
1 cup pecans finely chopped

Cream the butter and sugar. Add the water and vanilla. Add the flour and nuts. Roll the dough into the shape of dates but a bit larger. Bake at 300 degrees for about 30 minutes. Shake the cookies in powdered sugar after they have cooled slightly.

# Chocolate
# Decadence

Other things are just food. But chocolate's chocolate!

PATRICK SKENE CATLING

# Oatmeal Chocolate Chip Cookies

1 cup butter
1 cup brown sugar
1 cup sugar
2 eggs
1 teaspoon vanilla
2 cups flour
2½ cups blended oatmeal (Measure
   and blend to a fine powder in
   blender or food processor.)

½ teaspoon salt
1 teaspoon baking soda
1 teaspoon baking powder
2 cups (12 ounces) chocolate chips
1 4-ounce Hershey Bar, grated
1½ cups chopped walnuts

Cream butter with both sugars until fluffy. Add eggs and vanilla; mix together with flour, oatmeal, salt, baking soda, and baking powder. Add chocolate chips, grated Hershey Bar, and nuts. Roll into balls and place 2 inches apart on cookie sheet. Bake at 375 degrees for 10 minutes.

# Chunky Chocolate Cookies

*Sweeter and chunkier than the traditional chocolate chip cookie.*

1 4-ounce bar of sweet chocolate
1/2 cup butter
1/2 cup sugar
1/4 cup brown sugar
1 egg

1 teaspoon vanilla
1 cup all-purpose flour
1/2 teaspoon baking soda
1/2 teaspoon salt
1/2 cup coarsely chopped nuts

Chop chocolate bar into bite-sized pieces; set aside. Cream butter until soft. Add sugars, egg, and vanilla; beat until light and fluffy. Add flour, soda, and salt. Stir in chocolate pieces and nuts. Drop by teaspoonfuls 2 inches apart onto cookie sheet. Bake at 375 degrees for 8–10 minutes or until lightly browned.

# Grandmother's Oatmeal Raisin

(From the kitchen of Helen Fonti)

$^3/_4$ cup flour
$^1/_2$ teaspoon baking soda
$^1/_4$ teaspoon salt
$^1/_2$ cup butter
$^1/_2$ cup granulated sugar

$^1/_3$ cup packed brown sugar
1 large egg
2 teaspoons vanilla extract
$^1/_2$ cup uncooked oatmeal
$^3/_4$ cup dark seedless raisins

Combine flour, baking soda, and salt. In separate large bowl, beat butter and sugars until light and fluffy. Beat in egg and vanilla until well blended. Add in flour mixture; stir until well blended, but do not overbeat. Stir in oatmeal and raisins with wooden spoon. Drop heaping tablespoons of dough on ungreased cookie sheets. Bake at 350 degrees for 15 minutes.

# Cocoa Nut Drop Cookies

1 cup sugar
$\frac{1}{4}$ cup butter
1 egg
$\frac{1}{2}$ cup milk

1$\frac{1}{2}$ cups flour
2 teaspoons baking powder
$\frac{1}{2}$ cup cocoa
1 cup chopped nuts

Cream sugar and butter together. Beat egg, then add the egg and milk to sugar and butter mixture. Sift flour, baking powder, and cocoa. Add to mixture. Add nuts and stir well. Drop with spoon onto greased cookie sheet. Bake at 375 degrees for 15 minutes.

*A balanced diet is a cookie in each hand.*

AUTHOR UNKNOWN

# Chunky Peanut Butter Chocolate Chunk Cookies

(From the kitchen of Diane Pershing)

8 tablespoons (unsalted) butter
   at room temperature
1/4 cup granulated sugar
3/4 cup packed dark brown sugar
1 teaspoon vanilla extract
1/4 teaspoon salt
1/3 cup chunky-style peanut butter

1 egg
1/2 teaspoon baking soda
1 cup all-purpose flour
3/4 cup (about 4 ounces) coarsely
   chopped unsalted roasted peanuts
12 ounces (2 cups) coarsely chopped
   semisweet chocolate bars
   (4 3-ounce bars, such as Lindt
   or Tobler)
Vegetable shortening for baking sheets

Combine the butter, sugar, brown sugar, vanilla, and salt. Beat with a spoon until fluffy. Beat in the peanut butter, egg, and baking soda. Stir in the flour and then the peanuts and chocolate. Transfer to a bowl just large enough to hold the dough. Cover and refrigerate until firm, about 4 hours or overnight. Lightly coat 1 or 2 baking sheets with vegetable shortening. Using 1 tablespoon of dough for each cookie, shape the dough into balls. Place 12 cookies per sheet. Bake at 350 degrees for 10 minutes, until the cookies spring back when very lightly touched. Do not overbake or the cookies will dry out. Cool on the sheets for 2 minutes, then transfer to paper towel for about 2 minutes, and finally transfer to a rack to cool.

# Super Chocolate Icebox Cookies

*Rich and delicious!*

1¼ pounds of bittersweet
   chocolate, chopped
¾ cup unsalted butter
1⅓ cups sugar
4 large eggs

1 tablespoon vanilla
¾ cup flour
1½ cups semisweet chocolate
   chips

Line 8x8 pan with double layer of plastic wrap or waxed paper. Melt chocolate and butter in heavy saucepan, stirring constantly until smooth. Cool slightly. Whisk in sugar, then eggs and vanilla. Stir in flour. Stir in chocolate chips. Pour dough into prepared pan and smooth evenly. Cover with plastic and refrigerate overnight. Remove from pan and cut dough into 3 even bars (about $2\frac{1}{2}$x8 inches each). (If making ahead, wrap in plastic and place in freezer bag. Thaw in refrigerator overnight before continuing.) Line baking sheets with baking parchment or Exopat liners. Slice into $\frac{1}{2}$-inch thick slices and space about two inches apart. Bake at 350 degrees for about 15 minutes, or until puffed in center and wrinkled on top. Store in airtight container.

Tip: *Dough can be refrigerated or frozen to bake as needed.*

# Chocolate Crinkles

1 cup cocoa
2 cups granulated sugar
2 teaspoons vanilla
½ teaspoon salt
½ cup vegetable oil

4 eggs
2 cups flour
2 teaspoons baking powder
Powdered sugar

Combine ingredients, mixing well. Refrigerate overnight. Form balls and roll in powdered sugar. Bake at 350 degrees for 10–12 minutes. Sprinkle with powdered sugar after baking if desired.

# Bittersweet Chocolate Drops

4 ounces bittersweet chocolate,
   broken into pieces
2 tablespoons unsalted butter
½ cup granulated sugar

1 large egg
6 tablespoons flour
½ teaspoon baking powder

Coat a large baking sheet with cooking spray. In a medium saucepan over medium-low heat, stir the chocolate and butter until both are nearly melted. Remove from the heat and stir until the chocolate is completely melted. Blend in the sugar. Working quickly to prevent curdling, whisk in the egg. Stir in the flour and baking powder until stiff. Drop by rounded tablespoonfuls of dough about 1½ inches apart on cookie sheet. Bake at 350 degrees until the cookies are set and the tops are crackly, about 8–10 minutes. Let cool on the baking sheet for about 2 minutes before removing.

# Chocolate-Toffee Cookies

(From the kitchen of Andrea Schmidt)

2¼ cups flour
1 teaspoon baking soda
1 cup butter
¼ cup sugar
¾ cup brown sugar

1 teaspoon vanilla
1 small package vanilla
   instant pudding
2 eggs
12 ounces chocolate chips
½ bag toffee bits

Sift flour and baking soda. In separate bowl, mix butter, both sugars, vanilla, and vanilla pudding. Mix until smooth. Beat in eggs. Slowly add flour mixture. Stir in chocolate chips and toffee bits. Bake at 375 degrees for 8–10 minutes.

# Peanut Butter Chocolate Kiss Cookies

1/2 cup shortening
3/4 cup peanut butter
1/3 cup sugar
1/3 cup packed brown sugar
1 egg
2 tablespoons milk

1 teaspoon vanilla
1 1/3 cups flour
1 teaspoon baking soda
1/2 teaspoon salt
Extra sugar
1 package (6 ounces) Hershey's
   Kisses

Cream shortening and peanut butter. Add sugar and brown sugar. Add egg, milk, and vanilla. Beat well. Combine flour, baking soda, and salt. Gradually add creamed mixture and blend thoroughly. Shape dough into 1-inch balls; roll in sugar. Place on ungreased cookie sheet. Bake 10–12 minutes in 375-degree oven. Remove from oven immediately and place an unwrapped kiss on top of each cookie. Remove from cookie sheet and cool.

# Secret Kiss Cookies

(From the kitchen of Shelly Cassara)

1 cup butter, softened
½ cup granulated sugar
1 teaspoon vanilla extract
1¾ cups flour

1 cup finely chopped walnuts
1 bag (6 ounces) Hershey's Kisses
Powdered sugar

Beat butter, sugar, and vanilla until light and fluffy. Add flour and walnuts; mix well. Chill dough 1–2 hours. Remove wrappers from chocolate kisses. Use about 1 tablespoon of dough and shape around chocolate kiss. Roll to make ball. (Be sure to cover chocolate completely.) Bake at 375 for 10–12 minutes. While still slightly warm, roll in powdered sugar.

# Delicious Drop Cookies

Taste and see that the LORD is good.

PSALM 34:8

# Snickerdoodle Cookies

(From the kitchen of Vickie McDonough)

1 cup shortening (or ½ cup shortening and ½ cup butter)
1½ cups white sugar
2 eggs

1 teaspoon baking soda
¼ teaspoon salt
2¾ cups flour
2 teaspoons cream of tartar

**Coating:**
2 tablespoons sugar

2 teaspoons cinnamon

Mix shortening, sugar, and eggs. Add dry ingredients (except for coating). Roll into balls about 1-inch thick. Mix sugar and cinnamon coating and roll balls in the mixture. Place balls 2 inches apart on ungreased cookie sheet. Bake at 350 degrees for 8–10 minutes.

Tip: *Do not overbake. These cookies will not look like they are done at the end of 8–10 minutes. They will be very soft but will harden as they cool.*

*Nard and saffron, calamus and cinnamon,*
*with every kind of incense tree, with myrrh and*
*aloes and all the finest spices. . .*
SONG OF SONGS 4:14

# Butterfinger Cookies

¾ cup granulated sugar
½ cup butter, softened
1 large egg
1¾ cups all-purpose flour

¾ teaspoon baking soda
¼ teaspoon salt
1 cup (about 3 2.1-ounce
    bars) coarsely chopped
    Butterfinger Candy Bars

Beat sugar and butter in large mixer bowl until creamy. Beat in egg. Combine dry ingredients and gradually beat in egg mixture. Stir in Butterfinger pieces. Drop by slightly rounded tablespoons onto ungreased baking sheets. Bake at 375 degrees for 10–12 minutes or until lightly browned. Cool on baking sheets for 2 minutes before removing.

# Peanut Butter Cookies

1½ cups butter
1 cup sugar
1¼ cups peanut butter
   (smooth or chunky)
1 egg

½ teaspoon vanilla
½ teaspoon baking soda
1½ cups flour

Cream butter and sugar. Beat in peanut butter, egg, and vanilla. Mix in baking soda and flour. Roll dough into 1-inch balls and place on cookie sheet about 2 inches apart. Press flat with palm of hand or flatten and crisscross with a fork. Bake at 350 degrees for 10–12 minutes or until edges begin to brown.

# Lemon Cardamom Cookies

½ cup softened butter
½ cup light brown sugar
1 egg
2 cups flour

¼ teaspoon salt
¼ teaspoon ground cardamom seed
1¾ teaspoons grated lemon rind

Cream the butter and sugar until light and fluffy. Beat in egg. Mix together dry ingredients and stir into butter mixture. Knead dough briefly and chill. Roll into balls and flatten lightly. Bake at 350 degrees for 10–12 minutes or until the edges begin to brown.

*Something made with loving hands and*
*the finest ingredients tastes best.*

# Sugar-free Sweet Potato Raisin Cookies

1 cup raisins
1/4 cup butter
1 cup sweet potatoes,
   cooked and mashed
1 teaspoon vanilla
1 egg
2 cups whole wheat flour

1/4 teaspoon allspice
1/2 teaspoon salt
1/2 teaspoon nutmeg
1/2 teaspoon baking soda
1 teaspoon baking powder
1 teaspoon cinnamon
1/2 cup unprocessed bran flakes
1/4 cup chopped walnuts

Cover raisins with hot water and soak for 5 minutes, then drain. Cream butter. Add in sweet potatoes, vanilla, and egg; beat until creamy. In second bowl, mix flour, allspice, salt, nutmeg, baking soda, baking powder, and cinnamon. Gradually mix dry mixture into the creamed mixture. Mix well. Add in bran flakes and nuts. Stir. Add raisins last and stir gently. Drop onto greased cookie sheet. Bake at 350 degrees for 12 minutes.

# Applesauce Jumbles

(From the kitchen of Carolyn Kanow)
*The glaze on these cookies enhances the spices, making a yummy treat.*

2 eggs
½ cup shortening
1½ cups brown sugar
¾ cup applesauce
2 cups flour
1 teaspoon salt
½ teaspoon baking soda

1 teaspoon cinnamon
¼ teaspoon mace
¼ teaspoon cloves
1 cup raisins
1 cup chopped nuts
1 teaspoon vanilla

Cream eggs, shortening, sugar, and vanilla. Mix in applesauce. Add all dry ingredients. Cover and chill 2 hours. Drop round teaspoonfuls on ungreased cookie sheet. Bake at 375 degrees for 10 minutes or until there is no indentation when touched. Remove and cool before frosting.

**Brown Butter Glaze:**

| | |
|---|---|
| ½ cup margarine | 1½ teaspoons vanilla |
| 2 cups powdered sugar | 3–4 tablespoons hot water |

Heat margarine over low heat until golden brown. Remove from heat and add vanilla. Sift powdered sugar in and mix well with a whisk. Add water to desired consistency.

# Quick Cookies

(From the kitchen of Betty Young)

1 cup brown sugar
1 cup margarine or shortening
1 cup white sugar
2 eggs
¼ teaspoon baking powder
1 teaspoon vanilla

2 cups flour
3 cups cornflakes
1 teaspoon baking soda dissolved
    in 1 tablespoon water
¼ pound shredded coconut

Cream sugars and shortening; add eggs. Add all remaining ingredients. Drop on cookie sheet. Bake at 350 degrees for 8–10 minutes.

# Stir-and-Drop Sugar Cookies

(From the kitchen of Betty Young)

2 eggs
²/₃ cup oil
2 teaspoons vanilla
1 teaspoon grated lemon rind

³/₄ cup sugar
2 teaspoons baking powder
2 cups flour
½ teaspoon salt

Beat eggs and stir in oil, vanilla, and lemon. Blend in sugar and beat until thick. Add dry ingredients. Drop 2 inches apart on ungreased cookie sheet. Flatten with glass dipped in oil and sugar. Bake at 400 degrees for 8–10 minutes.

# Aggression Cookies

3 cups oatmeal                    1 ½ cups dark brown sugar
1 ½ cups self-rising flour        1 ½ cups butter

Dump all ingredients in a large bowl. Mash them! Knead them! Pound them! The longer and harder you mix the dough, the better it tastes. Roll dough into small balls. Bake on cookie sheet at 350 degrees for 10–12 minutes. They will be a little soft, but if they brown on bottom they are done. Cool on wire rack. Store in airtight container. They stay chewy.

Tip: *These also taste great if you use light brown sugar, 1 cup walnut pieces, and 6 ounces raisins!*

# Grandma Peggy's Molasses Cookies

*A family favorite—old-fashioned, timeless.*

²/₃ cup shortening
1 cup granulated sugar
1 egg
¼ cup molasses
2 cups flour

¼ teaspoon salt
½ teaspoon clove
2 teaspoons baking soda
1 teaspoon cinnamon
¾ teaspoon ginger

Cream shortening, sugar, and egg. Add molasses and mix well. Add dry ingredients. Roll dough into 1-inch balls and roll in sugar. Bake 375 for 10–12 minutes until they just flatten out. Watch them closely.

# Persimmon Cookies

½ cup shortening
1 cup sugar
1 egg
1 cup pureed persimmon pulp
2 cups flour
1 teaspoon baking soda
½ teaspoon nutmeg

1 teaspoon cinnamon
1 teaspoon baking powder
¼ teaspoon salt
¼ teaspoon clove
1 cup golden raisins
1 cup chopped nuts

Cream shortening, sugar, and egg. Add persimmon pulp and mix well. Add dry ingredients. Mix in raisins and nuts. Drop by teaspoonful onto ungreased cookie sheet. These cookies don't spread. Bake at 350 degrees for 12 minutes or until they just spring back when touched.

# Orange Cranberry Drops

| | |
|---|---|
| ½ cup white sugar | 1 teaspoon orange zest |
| ½ cup packed brown sugar | 1½ cups flour |
| ¼ cup butter, softened | ½ teaspoon baking powder |
| 1 egg | ¼ teaspoon baking soda |
| 3 tablespoons orange juice | ¼ teaspoon salt |
| ½ teaspoon orange extract | 1 cup dried cranberries |

Cream together the white sugar, brown sugar, and butter. Stir in the egg, orange juice, orange extract, and orange zest. Sift together the flour, baking powder, baking soda, and salt. Stir dry ingredients into the orange mixture. Fold in the dried cranberries. Drop heaping teaspoonfuls 2 inches apart on greased cookie sheet. Bake at 375 for 10–12 minutes or until edges begin to brown. Cool on baking sheets or remove to cool on wire racks.

# Pretty To Decorate—
# Roll and Press Cookies

The torch of love is lit in the kitchen.

FRENCH PROVERB

# Decorating Ideas

Kids love to help bake and decorate cookies. The holidays provide a wonderful opportunity to make memories that last a lifetime!

**Shape Them Up:**

Gather up all of your cookie cutters! No holiday cookie offering is complete without the charming, traditional figure of a gingerbread man or a temptingly iced tree.

Cookie presses have several interchangeable templates that also provide a variety of designs—from bars and butterflies to hearts and wreaths. In no time at all, you can press out dozens and dozens of picture-perfect cookies.

Free-form works, too! Check out the Candy Cane Twisties (pages 30–31) in which you can roll colored ropes of dough together to form delightful canes. Try Snowman Cookies (pages 22, 76–77, 132) in which the balls of dough create a jolly new friend. Our oh-so-quick and easy Butterscotch Haystacks (page 138) can be shaped to look like reindeer antlers. Use your imagination!

All for one, or one for all? Make up your mind—do you want to do an entire batch and fill a plate with one type of cookie, or would you rather offer an assortment of shapes and types in a basket?

Tip: *If the sizes of cookies vary significantly, as in the case of sugar cookies, bake cookies of the same size on the same sheet so smaller ones don't get too crisp.*

**Doll Them Up:**

Add a few drops of food coloring into the dough. Green makes pretty trees, holly leaves, and wreaths. A drop of yellow can make the lemon cookie look more vibrant.

Several recipes already feature recommended icings. For others, you can simply stir up a quick batch or open a commercially prepared cup. Use white, then divide it into small cups and add coloring as desired.

A cake-decorating paper or plastic cone with interchangeable tips adds a polished look to festive cookies.

You can also buy toothpaste-style tubes of already-colored icings that work beautifully. The gel tubes are easy to use and look wonderful, but a word of caution: They don't dry and are liable to smear!

Grab a variety of enhancements—chocolate chips, multicolored baking chips, M&Ms (both regular and minisized), red hots, gumdrops, licorice shoestrings, raisins, multiple colors of decorative sugar, jimmies, etc. During the holiday season, you can find little quarter-inch holly berry sprinkles with the cake decorations. Don't be afraid to try something a bit different. Part of a piece of candy corn makes a great nose for a snowman. Boston Baked Beans make terrific holly berries.

Crush peppermints or jewel-colored hard candies; then sprinkle on top of icing to give it extra sparkle and flavor.

**Stripe and Swipe:**

Ice a tree in white or pale green, then pipe or drizzle horizontal, dark green stripes. Take a knife or toothpick and stripe upward in the center from trunk to tip, forming boughs.

Spread white frosting over a simple circle, then add red striping around the edges—voila! A peppermint candy!

A giant square cookie can be iced, then decorated to become a giant Christmas card.

A quick, simple dusting of powdered sugar adds sweetness and a snowy look.

Pop a lollipop stick into a ball-shaped cookie, or sandwich a stick into the icing holding two sugar cookies back to back. Kids love these!

Tips: *When decorating cookies, always have graham crackers and pretzels around so you can use up the leftover icing to make graham sandwiches or dip the pretzels in the last bit of melted chocolate.*

*Tape a sheet of plastic to the table when decorating with children to make cleanup a bit easier. Kids, the cookies, or the table—it's hard to tell which one ends up wearing more sticky stuff. Be sure to take pictures!*

**Dish Them Out:**

Wrap an individual lollipop cookie with colored plastic wrap or cellophane and secure at the base with curling ribbon. If you didn't have lollipop sticks popsicle-type craft sticks work and can be personalized. Put one for each child of a family in a gift basket so each child will have something special all of his or her very own.

Wrap small, round or square tins, plastic ware, or Styrofoam with colored cellophane; bunch and tie cellophane on each side with pretty ribbons to make it look like a giant piece of hard candy.

Starch a doily heavily and drape it over the bottom of an overturned bowl until it's dry and stiff. Fill with shortbread and tie with tartan ribbon.

**Think of a Theme:**

Lemon Star Cookies on a golden or yellow plate; use a cellophane with tiny stars, and tie with golden ribbon. Snowmen and snowflakes work well, too.

Save peanut butter jars. Make cookies of a size that they stack and fill the jar perfectly. This can be especially fun if paired with a jar of homemade jelly.

Oversized coffee mugs, antique china cups and saucers, and whimsical trays are easy to fill and give away. It's fun to add sample-sized packets of gourmet coffee or tea to them.

Cellophane-wrap a batch of cookies and tuck it into a flower pot for an avid gardener. Tuck in a package of flower seeds, too.

**Make a List of Folks to Whom You'd Like to Give Cookies:**

Red Riding Hood wasn't wrong—Grandma loves getting a basket filled with cookies!

A single mother would love a jar mix to make with her kids.

Teachers and secretaries are delighted to find a decorated bag of cookies on their desks—fold over the top, punch two holes, and thread raffia or curling ribbon through the holes to make it festive.

The mail carrier would enjoy a decorated envelope brimming with them.

Mold scraps at the end of a batch into the shape of a bone for Fido.

# Sugar Cookies

⅔ cup butter
¾ cup sugar
1 egg
1 teaspoon vanilla

4 teaspoons milk
¼ teaspoon salt
1½ teaspoons baking powder
2 cups flour

Cream butter and sugar until fluffy. Blend in egg, vanilla, and milk. Combine dry ingredients and mix well. Divide dough in half and chill 1 hour. Roll dough ⅛-inch thick on lightly floured surface and cut with cookie cutters, or roll into tube and slice. Bake at 375 degrees for 6–8 minutes, or until edges begin to brown.

*Nothing is sweeter than Christ in your life.*

# Christmas Tree Spice Cookies

1 cup butter
1 cup sugar
1 large egg
½ cup honey
¾ teaspoon baking powder

2 teaspoons ground ginger
4½ cups flour
½ teaspoon salt
1 teaspoon cinnamon
Colored sugar sprinkles (optional)

Cream butter and sugar. Add egg and honey; continue beating until light and fluffy. Mix in dry ingredients (except colored sugar). Cover and chill dough for one hour. Roll out dough to ¼-inch thickness. Cut with 3–3½-inch tree-shaped cookie cutter. Place on lightly greased cookie sheet. Sprinkle with colored sugar. Bake at 375 for 10–12 minutes or until cookies are golden.

Tip: *Tree-shaped cookie cutters make this quick and simple!*

# Lemon Yummies

(From the kitchen of Sharon Kay Smith, who received
Cook, Hospitality, and Foods Girl Scout Badges with this recipe in 1955.)

| | |
|---|---|
| 1 cup shortening | 1 tablespoon grated lemon rind |
| ½ cup brown sugar | 2 cups flour |
| ½ cup granulated sugar | ½ teaspoon salt |
| 1 egg, well beaten | ¼ teaspoon baking soda |
| 2 tablespoons lemon juice | ½ cup chopped nut meats |

Cream the shortening, and add the sugars gradually. Add the egg, lemon juice, and rind, and mix well. Add the sifted dry ingredients and nut meats, and mix thoroughly. Form into a roll about 2 inches in diameter, wrap in waxed paper, and chill in the refrigerator. Cut into ¼-inch slices and bake on cookie sheets. Bake at 375 degrees for 8–10 minutes.

# Jolly Snowman Cookies

*This is so simple to do, and even the littlest helpers can be part of the fun.*
*Shoestring licorice turns into a snowman's top hat on these iced sugar cookies.*

**Directions:**

Using a favorite rolled cookie recipe, simply cut into circles with a cookie cutter, or roll dough and slice.

**Once cookies are cooled:**

1 tub of ready-to-spread frosting     ⅓ cup raisins
Black shoestring licorice     ¼ cup red cinnamon candies

**Ice cookies:**

Put frosting on each cookie. Cut licorice into pieces—some longer than others. Place licorice over top third of cookie to create hat. (Use longer pieces to create brim that overhangs cookie edges and shorter pieces to fit within cookie.) Use raisins for eyes and nose (1–3 pieces depending on cookie size) and 5 red candies for mouth.

Tip: *This is easiest if one cookie is frosted at a time and then decorated—especially for little fingers.*

# Holiday Iced Cookies

**Cookies:**

| | |
|---|---|
| ⅓ cup vegetable shortening | 1 teaspoon vanilla |
| ⅓ cup butter | 1 teaspoon baking powder |
| ¾ cup sugar | 2 cups flour |
| 1 egg | ¼ teaspoon salt |
| 1 tablespoon milk | |

Cream shortening, butter, sugar until fluffy. Add egg, milk, vanilla until combined. Combine dry ingredients and add slowly until well mixed. Divide dough in half. Cover and chill 3 hours or until dough is firm. On a lightly floured surface, roll ½ the dough to ⅛-inch thickness. Cut dough with cookie cutters into desired holiday shapes: stars, trees, bells, holly, etc. Bake at 375 degrees for 7–8 minutes or until edges are firm and bottoms are lightly browned.

**Icing:**
- 1 cup powdered sugar
- 1/4 teaspoon vanilla
- 1 tablespoon milk
- Food coloring (optional)

In a small mixing bowl stir powdered sugar, vanilla, and enough of the milk to make icing a piping consistency. Different-colored icings can be made by adding a few drops of food coloring. Use a pastry bag and writing tips to decorate cookies.

# Lemon Nut Star Cookies

*These are colorful, fun, and delicious, too! At Christmastime, use red and green food coloring and white (untinted) glaze for festive-looking cookies.*

**Cookies:**

| | |
|---|---|
| 1 cup butter, softened | 2 teaspoons grated lemon peel |
| 2 cups powdered sugar | 3¼ cups flour |
| 2 eggs | ½ cup finely ground almonds |
| 2 tablespoons lemon juice | ½ teaspoon baking soda |
| 4 teaspoons half-and-half cream | ⅛ teaspoon salt |

Cream butter and powdered sugar. Add eggs, one at a time. Beat well. Blend in lemon juice, cream, and lemon peel. Combine and gradually add flour, almonds, baking soda, and salt. Cover and refrigerate for 2–3 hours or until firm. On a lightly floured surface, roll dough to ⅛-inch thickness. Cut into stars with a cookie cutter. Bake at 350 degrees for 8–10 minutes or until lightly browned.

**Glaze:**

    2 cups powdered sugar           2 tablespoons lemon juice

    1/4 cup light corn syrup          Red and green food coloring

Stir powdered sugar, corn syrup, and lemon juice until smooth. Divide into 3 bowls. Tint one portion red, one green, and leave one plain. Spread over cookies. Allow to harden overnight.

Tip: *These make great Fourth of July cookies when iced with red, white, or blue glaze.*

# Filled Butterhorns

(From the kitchen of Shelly Cassara)

**Dough:**

4 cups flour
1 cup butter
4 egg yolks
2 yeast cakes

$\frac{1}{2}$ teaspoon salt
3 teaspoons sugar
2 cups sour cream

Combine flour and butter until crumbly. In another bowl, blend egg yolks, yeast, salt, sugar, and sour cream. Mix in flour and butter mixture immediately. Shape dough into small balls. Place on cookie sheet, cover with waxed paper, and chill overnight.

**Filling:**
    2 egg whites, beaten                    1 cup finely chopped walnuts
    ½ cup sugar

    Combine 2 egg whites and sugar; beat until stiff. Add nuts.

**To Assemble:**
    Roll each ball to ⅛-inch thick circle on lightly floured surface. Spoon filling onto circle and roll. Pinch ends and shape into horn (crescent).

**Topping:**
    1 egg white                         1 teaspoon light cream

    Blend together. Brush horns with egg white and cream mixture. Bake at 375 degrees for 20 minutes.

# Christmas Log Cookies

*A great rolled cookie!*

¾ cup shortening
¼ cup butter
1 cup powdered sugar
1¼ cups flour

½ teaspoon salt
2 teaspoons vanilla
1 cup oatmeal
Chopped nuts or coconut

Cream shortening, butter, and sugar until fluffy. Add flour, salt, vanilla, and oatmeal and mix well. Lay a piece of foil on the counter and sprinkle nuts or coconut on it. Shape dough into log and place on foil and pat nuts or coconut all around dough. Wrap dough and seal tightly. Refrigerate overnight or for up to a week. Slice and place on cookie sheet. Bake at 400 degrees for 7–8 minutes.

Tip: *Dough can be refrigerated or frozen and baked fresh when desired.*

# Mexican Christmas Cookies

| | |
|---|---|
| 2 tablespoons cinnamon | 1 cup fruit juice |
| 2 cups sugar | 2 egg yolks |
| 2 cups butter or shortening | 4 cups sifted flour |
| 1 tablespoon whole anise seed | |

In a large bowl, combine 1 tablespoon cinnamon and 1 cup of the sugar with the remaining ingredients. Stir until well blended. Chill covered for at least 1 hour; overnight is best. Roll dough out ¼-inch thick on a well-floured surface. Cut into 1-inch circles. Place on greased cookie sheet.

Bake at 350 degrees for 15 minutes, or until light brown. In a large bowl, combine the remaining sugar and cinnamon. Drop the warm cookies into the sugar mixture then place on a rack to cool.

# Eggnog Cookies

1 cup butter or margarine, softened
2 cups sugar
1 cup eggnog

1 teaspoon baking soda
½ teaspoon ground nutmeg
5½ cups flour

Beat butter and sugar until fluffy. Add eggnog, baking soda, and nutmeg, and mix well. Gradually add flour, mixing well. Divide dough in half; wrap in plastic. Chill overnight in refrigerator or 2 hours in freezer. On floured surface, roll out half of dough to ⅛-inch thickness. Cut out with flour-dipped cookie cutters. Place 1 inch apart on ungreased baking sheets. Bake at 375 degrees for 8–10 minutes or until lightly browned. Cool completely, then ice and decorate.

**Icing:**

    3 cups confectioners' sugar                    $^1/_3$ cup eggnog
    $^1/_4$ cup butter or margarine, softened

    Beat the confectioners' sugar and softened butter until well blended. Gradually beat in $^1/_3$ cup eggnog until icing is smooth.

# Shortbread

(From the kitchen of Vanessa Kealy, who received this recipe from a friend in Scotland. This is exactly the way she measured and prepared them.)

16 tablespoons flour—scoop & shake  
4 tablespoons sugar

8 tablespoons butter—1 cube set out a bit (margarine will not work)

Mix flour and sugar, then gradually squish in butter. Knead until dough forms a big ball. Flour board and roll out an 8x6-inch rectangle about 1/4-inch thick. Using a knife, cut into 2x1-inch strips. Place 1 inch apart on an ungreased baking sheet. Dip fork in flour and prick holes. Bake at 325 degrees, nice and slow. Check in 30–40 minutes. Bottom of shortbread will be pale brown. Remove from oven and let sit. Sprinkle with sugar.

# Shortbread Dainties

*These are lovely presented as a gift on a red plate tied with Tartan ribbon.*

$\frac{1}{2}$ cup butter
2 tablespoons confectioners' sugar
1 teaspoon vanilla

1 cup unbleached flour
1 cup finely chopped nuts
Confectioners' sugar

Cream butter and sugar together. Add vanilla and stir until light and fluffy. Stir in flour (or flour substitute). After flour is thoroughly blended in, add nuts. Form entire mixture into a 1-inch roll on waxed paper, twist shut, and refrigerate 1 hour. Cut into $\frac{1}{2}$-inch slices, then cut to form half circles. Place on ungreased cookie sheet. Bake at 300 degrees for 30–40 minutes until lightly browned. Roll in confectioners' sugar and let cool.

Tip: *If allergic to wheat, substitute $\frac{1}{2}$ cup potato flour and $\frac{1}{2}$ cup arrowroot.*

# Cottage Cheese Cookies

*Though they sound a bit unusual, these are melt-in-your-mouth delicious!*

1 cup cottage cheese
2 cubes butter
2 cups flour

3 tablespoons melted butter
$3/4$ cup brown sugar
$3/4$ cup chopped walnuts

Blend together cottage cheese and cubed butter, then add flour. Roll out into a $1/8$-inch-thick circle on floured board. Spread with melted butter. Sprinkle with brown sugar and walnuts. Cut pie-style, then roll from large to small end of wedge like a croissant. Bake at 400 degrees for 10 minutes. Store in sealed tin in refrigerator.

# Swedish Tea Cookies

(From the kitchen of Tracie Peterson)
*Give these in a basket and fill with special tins of tea and honey.*
*And maybe a teacup, too!*

1 cup butter
2 cups brown sugar
2 eggs

3 $\frac{1}{2}$ cups flour, sifted
1 teaspoon baking soda
$\frac{1}{2}$ teaspoon salt
1 cup chopped nuts

Cream the butter and sugar. Add the eggs. Sift the flour with the baking soda and salt. Add the nuts. Roll into a tube. Chill for at least 2 hours. Slice thinly. Bake at 350 degrees for 7–10 minutes.

## Moravian Scotch Cakes

4 cups flour                                    ½ cup sugar
2 teaspoons caraway seeds            1½ cups butter

Mix the flour, caraway seeds, and sugar together. Work the butter in with your fingertips until well blended. Roll out about ⅓-inch thick on well-floured board. Cut into small squares and place on greased cookie sheet. Bake at 325 degrees for about 15 minutes. Do not overbake. When cool, decorate with icing and sprinkle with colored sugar.

# Sour Cream Spritz

1 cup butter
¾ cup sugar
1 egg yolk
⅓ cup sour cream
1 teaspoon vanilla

¾ teaspoon cinnamon
¼ teaspoon baking soda
2¾ cups flour, sifted
½ teaspoon salt

Cream butter and sugar well. Beat in egg yolk, sour cream, and vanilla. Sift dry ingredients and gradually blend into butter mixture. Using cookie press, form cookies on ungreased sheets. Bake at 375 degrees for 8–10 minutes.

# Spritz

| | |
|---|---|
| 1½ cups butter | 1 teaspoon almond extract |
| 1 cup sugar | 1 teaspoon baking powder |
| 1 egg | ¼ teaspoon salt |
| 1 teaspoon vanilla | 4 cups sifted all-purpose flour |

Cream butter until very soft. Work in sugar, then egg and vanilla. Sift together dry ingredients and add to first mixture gradually. Form cookies with cookie press on ungreased cookie sheet. Decorate with decorating sugars, chopped cherries, and/or nuts. Bake at 400 degrees for 8–10 minutes.

Tip: *Refrigerate ungreased cookie sheets until ready to use.*

# Vanilla Cookies

*A touch of cardamom makes these cookies extraspecial.*

| | |
|---|---|
| 1 cup unsalted butter, softened | ½ teaspoon ground cardamom |
| 1 cup sugar | ½ teaspoon salt |
| 1 large egg | 2½ cups flour |
| 2½ teaspoons vanilla extract | Vanilla sugar (optional) |

Beat butter and sugar until light and fluffy. Beat in egg, vanilla, cardamom, and salt. Mix in flour. Pack dough into cookie press. Fit with desired design plate. Space cookies 1 inch apart on ungreased cookie sheet. Bake at 375 degrees about 10 minutes or until golden brown. Gently transfer cookies to wire racks. If desired, sprinkle with vanilla sugar. Store in airtight container.

Tip: *Place vanilla bean cut lengthwise in 1 cup sugar and store tightly for a day or two. This is also delightful to add to coffees.*

# Brown Sugar Cookies

*Not too sweet—perfect with coffee or tea.*

2 cups light brown sugar
1 cup melted butter
3 eggs
¼ cup milk

1 tablespoon vanilla
1 teaspoon baking soda
5 to 5½ cups flour—
     enough to make mixture stiff

Mix ingredients in order given. Add just enough flour to make dough firm enough to roll. Cut into shapes as desired. Decorate with colored sugars, frosting, or sprinkle lightly with brown sugar. Bake at 350 degrees for 8–10 minutes or until edges are lightly browned.

Tip: *This recipe works well with cookie cutters or a cookie press.*

# Lemon Butter Cookies

1 pound unsalted butter, softened
1 cup sugar
6 egg yolks
1 tablespoon vanilla

2 drops yellow food coloring
Zest of 2 lemons
5 cups all-purpose flour
1 egg

Cream together butter and sugar. Add egg yolks, vanilla, food coloring, and lemon zest and mix well. Gradually add flour while stirring. Chill for 1 hour. Roll out $1/4$-inch thick and cut in shapes desired. Beat remaining egg; brush each cookie with beaten egg. Place on parchment-lined baking sheet. Bake at 325 degrees for 24 minutes or until lightly golden.

# Lemon Cinnamon Cookies

4 cups all-purpose flour
2 cups sugar
1 tablespoon ground cinnamon
1 teaspoon cream of tartar
1 teaspoon baking soda
1/2 teaspoon salt
1 cup unsalted butter

3 beaten eggs
2 teaspoons finely shredded
    lemon peel
1 egg white
1 tablespoon water
Sugar
4 ounces semisweet chocolate
    pieces, melted

In a very large mixing bowl, stir together the flour, 2 cups sugar, cinnamon, cream of tartar, baking soda, and salt. Cut in butter until mixture looks like cornmeal. Add eggs and lemon peel; mix well to form a dough. On a floured surface, roll dough to 1/8-inch thickness. Cut into shapes with cookie cutters. Place on ungreased cookie sheets. Combine egg white and water; brush over tops of cookies. Sprinkle cookies with sugar. Bake at 375 degrees for 8–10 minutes until golden. Remove to wire rack to cool. Drizzle melted chocolate over them.

# Bountiful Bars

It was white like coriander seed and
tasted like wafers made with honey.

EXODUS 16:31

# King Gustav Cookies

2 sticks of butter, softened
1 cup sugar
1 large egg, divided into yolk
   and egg white

1 cup all-purpose flour
1 teaspoon imitation brandy extract
Diced, sliced, or chopped
   pecans

First cream butter with mixer. Gradually add granulated sugar a little at a time; cream well. Add egg yolk and cream with above; add sifted flour a little at a time. Add extract. Divide dough evenly in 2 parts and lightly grease 2 16x11x1-inch pans all over. Put dough on pans, and spread evenly, quite thin (12–13 ounces each pan). Put some of the egg white on top of each batter, rubbing the egg white on top of each batter with the palm of the hand. Pour off excess egg white (egg white should be moved around the top of the batter until smooth and shiny). Sprinkle pecans over batter. Bake 55 minutes in a 250-degree oven (preheated), or at 325 degrees for 15 to 20 minutes. Check after 25 minutes, as cookies bake faster in a gas oven. Cookies should be a light brownish color before removing from oven. Cut into squares as soon as cookies are removed from oven. Let cool for 1 hour before removing cookies from pan.

# Frosted Banana Bars

(From the kitchen of Vickie McDonough)

$\frac{1}{2}$ cup butter or margarine, softened
$1\frac{1}{2}$ cups sugar
2 eggs
1 cup (8 ounces) sour cream
1 teaspoon vanilla extract

2 cups all-purpose flour
1 teaspoon baking soda
$\frac{1}{4}$ teaspoon salt
2 medium ripe bananas, mashed
   (about 1 cup)

In a mixing bowl, cream butter and sugar. Add eggs, sour cream, and vanilla. Combine flour, baking soda, and salt; gradually add to the creamed mixture. Stir in bananas. Spread into a greased 15x10x1-inch baking pan. Bake at 350 degrees for 20–25 minutes or until a toothpick inserted near the center comes out clean. Cool.

**Frosting:**
   1 package (8 ounces)
      cream cheese, softened
   ½ cup butter or margarine

   2 teaspoons vanilla extract
   3¾–4 cups powdered sugar

In a mixing bowl beat cream cheese, butter, and vanilla. Gradually beat in enough powdered sugar to achieve desired consistency. Frost bars. Store in the refrigerator.

# Brown Sugar Chews

1 egg
1 cup packed brown sugar
1 teaspoon vanilla
½ cup sifted flour

¼ teaspoon salt
¼ teaspoon baking soda
1 cup chopped walnuts

Stir together egg, brown sugar, and vanilla. Add flour, salt, and baking soda. Fold in walnuts. Bake at 350 degrees for 18–20 minutes in well-greased 8x8-inch pan. Should be soft when removed from the oven. Cool in pan, then cut into squares.

# Cream Cheese Bars

*Like cheesecake? These are a dream!*

1 stick butter
1 box golden yellow cake mix
1 pound box confectioners' sugar

2 eggs
1 package (8 ounces) cream cheese

Mix butter and cake mix until crumbly. Spread in buttered 9x13-inch pan. Cream confectioners' sugar, eggs, and cream cheese. Spread over cake mix crust. Bake at 350 degrees for 35 minutes. Watch carefully—these bars burn easily.

*"He will provide delicacies fit for a king."*

GENESIS 49:20

# Smitty's Pineapple Bars

1 tablespoon butter
1 tablespoon sugar
1 cup flour
1/4 teaspoon salt
3 teaspoons baking powder

3 well-beaten eggs
1 cup drained, crushed pineapple
1 cup sugar
1 tablespoon melted butter
2 cups shredded coconut

Cream butter and 1 tablespoon sugar. Sift flour with salt and baking powder and add to butter. Add 1/2 of the eggs; mix well. Pour into greased 8x8-inch pan. Spread with pineapple. Mix 1 cup sugar, melted butter, and coconut. Add remaining eggs and mix well. Spread over pineapple. Bake at 350 degrees for 30 minutes. Cool and cut into squares.

# Gumdrop Cookies

4 eggs, separated
2 cups brown sugar
1 teaspoon vanilla
½ cup chopped nuts
1 cup finely cut orange gumdrops
   (Assorted flavors are okay, but
   remove the licorice ones.)

1 tablespoon water
2 cups flour
½ teaspoon salt
1 teaspoon baking powder

Spray 9x13-inch pan with nonstick spray, line with waxed paper, and spray waxed paper. Beat egg yolks until light and lemon colored. Add the sugar and beat well. Add vanilla. Add nuts, gumdrops, and water. Sift flour, salt, and baking powder twice. Gradually add dry ingredients to mixture. Beat egg whites until stiff. Gently fold into bowl. Pour into pan. Bake at 350 degrees for 25 minutes. While still warm, drizzle with icing made of 1½ cups confectioners' sugar, 3 tablespoons butter, and 2 tablespoons orange juice.

# Chocolate Trio Squares

*These only sound complicated—they go together fast and look impressive.*

**Layer 1:**

Cream together and spread in greased and floured 9x9-inch pan:

¼ cup butter                                    1 cup sifted flour
¼ teaspoon salt

Bake at 350 degrees for 15 minutes.

**Layer 2:**

2 eggs                                          ¼ cup brown sugar
Beat together well, then add:

| 1 cup finely chopped walnuts | ½ cup shredded coconut |
| 1 teaspoon vanilla | ¼ teaspoon salt |
| 2 tablespoons flour | |

Spread over first baked layer. Bake at 350 degrees for 15 minutes. Cool in pan.

**Layer 3 (icing):**

| 1 cup semisweet chocolate chips | 1 tablespoon water |
| ¼ cup light corn syrup | Chopped nuts |

Melt chocolate chips in microwave; add ¼ cup light corn syrup and 1 tablespoon water. Spread over second layer. Sprinkle with chopped nuts if desired.

## Butterscotch Squares

¼ cup butter
1 cup packed brown sugar
1 egg
½ teaspoon vanilla

1 cup flour
½ teaspoon salt
1 teaspoon baking powder
½ cup blanched almond halves

Cream butter, brown sugar, egg, and vanilla. Sift dry ingredients. Add dry ingredients into mixture. Spread in greased 8x8-inch pan. Top with almonds. Bake at 350 degrees for 30–35 minutes. Cool, then cut into squares.

# Fruit Squares

2 eggs
1 cup brown sugar
2 teaspoons vanilla
1 teaspoon baking powder
1 cup cake flour

½ teaspoon salt
⅔ cup chopped nuts
1 cup candied fruit, chopped
1 cup dried fruit (dates, citron,
    raisins, figs) chopped

Beat eggs until they start to stiffen. Gradually beat in sugar and add vanilla. Sift dry ingredients together and add. Fold in chopped nuts and the fruit. Pour in 8x8-inch pan that is generously sprayed with nonstick spray. Bake at 350 degrees for 30–40 minutes. Remove from pan while warm. Cool and cut into 1-inch squares.

## Brownies

1 cup sugar
½ cup butter
2 eggs
½ cup milk
⅔ cup sifted flour

½ teaspoon baking powder
1 cup nut meats
2 squares baking chocolate
1 teaspoon vanilla

Mix ingredients in the order given. Pour into greased pan. Bake at 350 degrees for 25 minutes.

**Icing:**

1 cup brown sugar

1 1/2 tablespoons butter

Pinch of salt

1/4 cup milk

1 1/2 cups powdered sugar

1 teaspoon vanilla

2 tablespoons cocoa

Combine brown sugar, butter, salt, and milk. Bring to boil and cook slowly for 3 minutes. Cool to lukewarm. Add powdered sugar, vanilla, and cocoa. Beat until smooth and spreadable.

# One Bowl Bar Cookies

*Pressed for time? This recipe doesn't take much time or cleanup.*

1 package applesauce-raisin cake mix
¾ cup quick oats
¼ cup wheat germ
½ cup light molasses
¼ cup orange juice

2 eggs
2 tablespoons vegetable oil
½ cup raisins
½ cup flaked coconut

Combine cake mix, oats, and wheat germ. Add molasses, orange juice, eggs, and oil. Stir until well blended, then add raisins and coconut. Spread in greased jelly-roll pan. Bake at 375 degrees for 20 minutes (lightly browned and pulled away from pan's edge). Cool. Ice with Orange Glaze before cutting.

**Orange Glaze:**
2 cups confectioners' sugar                    $\frac{1}{4}$– $\frac{1}{3}$ cup orange juice

Blend together until thin enough to pour but thick enough to spread.

# Lemon Bars

(From the kitchen of Angela Boone-Guzman)

**Crust:**
> ½ cup butter
> ¼ cup powdered sugar
> 1 cup flour

Cream butter and sugar until fluffy. Add flour and mix well. Spread in 8x8-inch greased pan. Bake at 350 degrees for 12 minutes.

**Second layer:**

| | |
|---|---|
| 1 cup sugar | 1/4 teaspoon salt |
| 2 beaten eggs | 2 tablespoons flour |
| 4 tablespoons lemon juice | 1/2 teaspoon baking powder |

Beat sugar and eggs, adding in lemon juice. Add dry ingredients and mix well. Spread over crust, covering all edges. Bake at 350 degrees for 30 minutes. Cool and dust with powdered sugar. Cut in 1x2-inch rectangles.

Tip: *Angela's Swedish great-grandmother substituted potato flour for the wheat flour and always creamed the butter for a full 5 minutes until it was light and fluffy.*

# Apricot Bars

$^2/_3$ cup dried apricots
$^1/_2$ cup soft butter or margarine
$^1/_4$ cup granulated sugar
$1^1/_3$ cups flour
2 well-beaten eggs

$^1/_2$ teaspoon vanilla
$^1/_2$ teaspoon baking powder
1 cup packed brown sugar
$^1/_2$ teaspoon salt

Rinse apricots, then cover with water and boil for 10 minutes. Drain and set aside. Mix butter, granulated sugar, and 1 cup flour together with a fork until crumbly. Pat into greased 8x8-inch pan. Bake at 350 degrees for 25 minutes or until lightly browned. Meanwhile, mix the following ingredients together, adding only one item at a time:

| | |
|---|---|
| Eggs | Brown sugar |
| Vanilla | Salt |
| Baking powder | $\frac{1}{3}$ cup flour |

Add apricots. Spread over baked layer and bake another 30 minutes. Wait until cool to cut into bars.

# Gingersnap Bars

¾ cup shortening
1 cup sugar
1 teaspoon cinnamon
½ teaspoon ginger
¼ cup molasses
2 cups all-purpose flour

2 teaspoons baking soda
½ teaspoon cloves
½ teaspoon salt
1 egg
2 tablespoons sugar

Melt shortening in large saucepan; cool 5 minutes. Add remaining ingredients except 2 tablespoons sugar; mix well. Press in bottom of greased 15x10-inch jelly-roll pan. Sprinkle with remaining sugar. Bake at 375 degrees for 10–12 minutes. Do not overbake. After 5 minutes, cut into bars. Cool completely.

# Cranberry Crunch Squares

1 (16-ounce) can jellied cranberry sauce
2⅓ cups rolled oats
¾ cup all-purpose flour

1⅝ cups packed brown sugar
1 cup butter, melted

Spread the cranberry sauce into the bottom of a greased 9x13-inch baking pan. Stir oats, flour, brown sugar, and butter until the mixture resembles coarse crumbs. Sprinkle crumb mixture over cranberry sauce. Bake at 350 degrees for 25 minutes. Cool and cut into squares.

# Marvelous Meringues and Macaroons

"Listen, listen to me, and eat what is good,
and your soul will delight in the richest of fare."

ISAIAH 55:2

# French Coconut Macaroons

*With crisp-chewy outsides and soft centers,*
*these are popular with children* and *grown-ups!*

4 egg whites
1 teaspoon pure vanilla extract
1 cup powdered sugar

2 cups flaked coconut
½ cup flour

Beat egg whites until stiff peaks form. Add vanilla and mix well. Gradually add in powdered sugar, beating well after each addition. Beat until stiff and glossy. Fold in coconut and flour until well mixed. Drop by teaspoonfuls onto lightly buttered and floured cookie sheet. Bake at 325 degrees for 25 minutes or until lightly browned.

# Sweet as Angel's Kisses

4 egg whites, room temperature
$\frac{1}{4}$ teaspoon cream of tartar
$\frac{1}{8}$ teaspoon salt

1 cup sugar
$\frac{1}{4}$ teaspoon peppermint extract
A few drops of red food coloring

Beat egg whites until foamy. Add cream of tartar and salt; beat until soft peaks form. Add sugar, beating until stiff peaks form. Mix in peppermint extract and food coloring. Drop rounded tablespoons of mixture onto parchment paper or foil-lined cookie sheets. Bake at 250 degrees for 35–45 minutes or until cookies are firm to the touch and just beginning to brown around the edges. Remove from oven and cool.

# Pecan Kisses

*A Christmas favorite!*

| | |
|---|---|
| 2 large egg whites | ½ teaspoon vanilla extract |
| ¾ cup light brown sugar | 2 cups pecan halves or pieces |

Beat egg whites until stiff peaks form. Gradually beat in brown sugar and vanilla until well blended. Fold in pecans until coated. Drop by teaspoonfuls onto nonstick cookie sheet about 1 inch apart. Bake at 250 degrees for 30 minutes. Turn oven off; let stand in closed oven another 30 minutes. Don't open oven door! Remove from oven and cool on wire rack. Store in airtight container.

Tip: *These cookies freeze well.*

# Amnesia Cookies

2 egg whites                    1 cup chopped nuts
²⁄₃ cup sugar                    1 cup chocolate chips

Preheat oven to 350 degrees. Beat eggs until fluffy. Gradually add sugar. Beat until stiff. Stir in nuts and chocolate chips. Drop on foil-lined pan. Put in oven and close door. **Turn oven off!** Do not open oven door until morning!

*Kissing don't last: cookery do.*

GEORGE MEREDITH

# All-Night Kisses

2 egg whites
Dash of salt

¾ cup sugar
1 6-ounce package of butterscotch, chocolate, or mint chocolate chips

Preheat oven to 350 degrees. Beat egg whites and salt until stiff. Gradually add sugar. Fold in flavored chips. Drop by teaspoonfuls onto ungreased cookie sheet—these stay in shape they are dropped, so form into candy kiss shape. Put in oven and close door. **Turn oven off!** Do not open oven door until morning!

# Amaretti

*These almond macaroons are an Italian favorite.*

2 egg whites
1 teaspoon vanilla
½ teaspoon almond extract
1½ cups blanched almonds, finely chopped (about 8 ounces)
1 cup powdered sugar, sifted

Beat egg whites, vanilla, and almond extract until stiff peaks form. Combine almonds and powdered sugar, then fold into egg white mixture. Drop by teaspoonfuls onto greased cookie sheet (or on cookie sheet lined with parchment paper). Bake at 325 degrees for 15–20 minutes, until lightly browned. For crisper cookies, turn off oven, open door, and let dry for another 10–15 minutes.

# Oh-So-Quick and Easy

Do what you can, with what you have, where you are.

THEODORE ROOSEVELT

# Easy Chocolate Chip Cookies

*This is a quick and simple treat and something kids can do, too.*
*Chocolate cake mixes work well for a double fudge taste!*

1 package white cake mix
½ cup nuts
1 egg

¼ cup light brown sugar
¾ cup oil
1 cup (6 ounces) chocolate chips

Mix first five ingredients well. Stir in chocolate chips. Drop by rounded teaspoonfuls onto cookie sheet. Bake at 375 degrees for 10–12 minutes.

# Easy Oatmeal Cookies

*Chewy and crispy! This is so kid-friendly, children can mix it with their hands!*

1 cup butter, softened
1 cup flour
1 teaspoon baking soda

1 cup sugar
2 cups oats

Mix all ingredients together. Dough will form a large ball. Roll into small balls and flatten. Bake at 350 degrees for 12–14 minutes.

# Snowmen Cookies

*No time to bake? Try this simple and decorative alternative!*
*Great for gifts, too!*

1 package (16 ounces)
 Nutter Butter cookies
1¼ pounds white candy coating,
 melted
Licorice strings

Miniature chocolate chips
M&M miniature baking bits
Pretzel sticks, halved
Orange and red frosting

Using tongs, dip cookies into candy coating. Shake off excess. Place on waxed paper. Using pieces of licorice, create hat on upper portion of cookie. Place two chocolate chips for eyes. Place baking bits down lower half of cookie for buttons. For arms, dip ends of pretzel stick halves into coating; attach one to each side. Let stand until hardened. Pipe nose with orange frosting. Pipe scarf at indented point with red frosting.

# Buckeyes

(From the kitchen of Carolyn Boone)
*These disappear fast!*

**Filling:**

    2 pounds peanut butter              1 pound butter
    3 pounds powdered sugar

    Mix well. Chill until firm. Roll into 1-inch balls.

**Icing:**

    2 packages chocolate chips (12 ounces) ½ bar paraffin wax

    Melt in double boiler. Using toothpick, dip balls in chocolate, leaving just the top uncovered. Cool on waxed paper.

Tip: *Buckeyes are best made with a heavy-duty mixer.*

# Grandma Dabb's No-Bake Graham Cracker Cookies

(From the kitchen of Sharon Kealy)

Mix the following ingredients in saucepan:

$2/3$ cup milk                                    1 cup sugar

Boil for 3 minutes and remove from heat.

**Add:**
1 teaspoon vanilla                          6 tablespoons peanut butter

Mix into this $1/4$ pound graham crackers that have been crushed. Stir until completely heated through and drop by spoonfuls on waxed paper.

# Lemon Snowflake Cookies

1 package lemon cake mix
  with pudding
1 egg

2¼ cups frozen whipped topping,
  thawed
2 cups powdered sugar

Mix the cake mix, egg, and whipped topping together. Beat with an electric mixer on medium speed until well blended and sticky. Drop one teaspoonful batter into the powdered sugar and roll to coat. Place cookies onto ungreased sheets. Bake at 350 degrees for 8–10 minutes or until lightly browned.

# Super Easy Peanut Butter Cookies

(From the kitchen of Betty Young)
*No flour, salt, or anything. Enjoy!*

1 cup peanut butter (crunchy or creamy)          1 cup sugar
1 egg

Mix all together well. Roll into about 1-inch balls, then crisscross with fork. Bake at 350 degrees for about 10 minutes or until golden brown.

# Chocolate Orange Balls

*A quick, easy, no-bake recipe.*

1 9-ounce box of vanilla wafer cookies
2 1/4 cups confectioners' sugar
1/4 cup unsweetened cocoa powder
1/3 cup orange juice concentrate

1/4 cup light corn syrup
1 teaspoon water
1 1/2 cups nuts (Almonds, hazel nuts, or pecans work best.)

Combine the vanilla wafers, 2 cups of the confectioners' sugar, cocoa powder, orange juice concentrate, and corn syrup in a food processor. Process until the cookies are ground to crumbs and mixture is evenly blended. If the mixture looks too dry, add water a few drops at a time and blend. Add the nuts and process on "pulse" until the nuts are finely chopped. Transfer the mixture to a bowl and form into 1-inch balls. Roll balls in 1/4 cup confectioners' sugar to coat. Store in refrigerator in an airtight container for up to 1 month.

# Butterscotch Haystacks

*These are really cute when shaped into reindeer antlers.*

1 cup creamy peanut butter                    1 large can chow-mein noodles
6 ounces butterscotch chips

Melt peanut butter and butterscotch together on the stovetop or in a micro-wave. Pour over noodles and quickly mix well. Drop by tablespoon on waxed paper. Freeze for a couple of hours. Store at room temperature in a cookie jar.

# Triple Chocolate Chip Cookies

1 box chocolate cake mix (2-layer size)
1 box instant chocolate pudding
   (4-serving size)
1 cup sour cream
1 cup chocolate chips
2 large eggs

Combine all five ingredients in the bowl. Stir until moistened and no big lumps remain. Drop by rounded spoonfuls, about 2 inches apart, onto greased cookie sheet. Bake at 350 degrees for 16–18 minutes. Let stand 2 minutes. Cool completely.

# Praline Cookies

12 graham crackers, broken
   into quarters
1 cup light brown sugar

1 cup butter
1 cup pecan pieces or sliced
   almonds

Line a baking sheet with aluminum foil and place quarters of graham crackers on it, spaced a little bit apart. Bring brown sugar and butter to a boil and heat into soft-ball stage on a candy thermometer—about 2 minutes after the mixture comes to a full boil. Remove from heat and add pecan pieces or almonds. Pour over the graham crackers and spread nuts evenly among cookies. Bake cookies at 350 degrees for 10 minutes. The mixture will have softened again. Separate into cookies and cool on brown paper. Makes about 48 cookies.

# Mason-Jar Cookie Mixes for Gift-Giving

I wish we could put up some of the Christmas spirit

in jars and open a jar of it every month.

HARLAN MILLER

# Cherry Jubilee Cookies

½ cup plus 2 tablespoons flour
½ cup rolled oats
½ cup flour mixed with ½ teaspoon
    baking soda
½ teaspoon salt

⅓ cup white sugar
⅓ cup plus 1 tablespoon
    packed brown sugar
½ cup dried cherries
½ cup slivered almonds

Layer the ingredients in a quart jar in order as listed. Attach recipe that follows to jar:

**Cherry Jubilee Cookies:**

In a medium bowl, cream together:
½ cup butter                                    1 egg
1 teaspoon vanilla

Add the entire jar of ingredients. Mix together by hand until well blended. Drop by heaping spoonfuls onto greased baking sheet. Bake at 350 degrees for 8–10 minutes.

# Blueberry Hazelnut Dreams

½ cup plus 2 tablespoons flour
½ cup rolled oats
½ cup flour mixed with
  ½ teaspoon baking soda
½ teaspoon salt

⅓ cup plus 1 tablespoon
  packed brown sugar
⅓ cup white sugar
½ cup hazelnut pieces
½ cup dried blueberries

Layer the ingredients in a quart jar in order as listed. Attach recipe that follows to jar:

**Blueberry Hazelnut Dreams:**

In a medium bowl, cream together:
½ cup butter                          1 egg
1 teaspoon vanilla

Add the entire jar of ingredients. Mix together by hand until well blended. Drop by heaping spoonfuls onto greased baking sheet. Bake at 350 degrees for 8–10 minutes.

# Polka Dot Oatmeal Cookies

½ cup packed brown sugar
¼ cup white sugar
¾ cup wheat germ
1 cup quick-cooking oats
¼ cup dried cherries
½ cup raisins

⅔ cup packed flaked coconut
¼ cup dried cranberries
1 cup flour
½ teaspoon salt
½ teaspoon baking soda

Layer ingredients in order given in a quart jar. Attach recipe that follows to jar:

**Polka Dot Oatmeal Cookies:**

Empty the jar into a large bowl. Blend mixture well before adding: ½ cup of softened butter. Mix until mixture resembles coarse crumbs. In separate bowl, beat together:

1 egg                                    1 teaspoon vanilla
¼ cup milk

Blend egg mixture into the dough until well combined. Bake on greased cookie sheet at 350 degrees for 10–14 minutes.

# Brownies by the Quart

Layer in a one-quart jar:

2 ¼ cups white sugar
⅔ cup cocoa
½ cup chopped nuts

1 ¼ cups flour
1 teaspoon baking powder
1 teaspoon salt

Attach recipe that follows to jar:

**Brownies by the Quart:**

Empty mix into large bowl. Mix thoroughly. In a small bowl, mix:

¾ cup of butter
4 slightly beaten eggs

Add butter and egg mixture to dry ingredients and stir well with fork. Spread batter into a lightly greased 9x13-inch pan. Bake at 350 degrees for 30 minutes or until done.

# Chunky Chocolate Macadamias

Layer in a wide-mouthed one-quart jar:

$^3/_4$ cup brown sugar (Pack firmly in jar.) $^1/_2$ cup white sugar
$^1/_4$ cup unsweetened cocoa powder $^1/_2$ cup chopped macadamias
   (Wipe any smears off inside jar.) 1 cup jumbo chocolate chips
$1^3/_4$ cups flour 1 teaspoon baking soda
1 teaspoon baking powder $^1/_4$ teaspoon salt

Attach recipe that follows to jar:

**Chunky Chocolate Macadamias:**

Empty jar of cookie mix into a large mixing bowl. Mix dry ingredients with spoon. Add:

| | |
|---|---|
| ¾ cup butter softened at room temperature. (Margarine does not work.) | 1 egg, slightly beaten<br>1 teaspoon vanilla |

Mix until completely blended. The dough is thick and sticky. You'll need to finish mixing with your hands. Shape into walnut-size balls and place 2 inches apart on parchment-lined baking sheets. Do not use waxed paper. Bake at 350 degrees for 11–13 minutes. Cool 5 minutes on baking sheet. Remove to racks to finish cooling.

# Peanut Butter and Chocolate Cookie Jar Mix

Layer in a one-quart jar:

¾ cup sugar

1¾ cups flour

½ teaspoon baking soda

½ cup brown sugar

1 teaspoon baking powder

8 Reeses' peanut butter cups,
chopped into chunks

Attach recipe that follows to jar:

**Peanut Butter and Chocolate Cookies:**

Sift out the peanut butter cup chunks and set aside. Empty remaining cookie mix into large mixing bowl and stir with fork. Add:

½ cup butter softened at room temperature   1 egg, slightly beaten
1 teaspoon vanilla

Mix until completely blended. Mix in peanut butter cup chunks. Shape into 1½-inch balls. Place 2 inches apart on greased cookie sheets. Bake at 375 degrees for 12–14 minutes. Cool 5 minutes on baking sheet. Remove cookies to racks to finish cooling.

# Cowboy Cookie Mix

Layer in a 1-quart jar:

1⅓ cups quick oats
½ cup sugar
1 cup chocolate chips
1 teaspoon baking powder
2 dashes salt

½ cup firmly packed brown sugar
½ cup chopped pecans
1⅓ cups flour mixed with
    1 teaspoon baking soda

Attach recipe that follows to jar:

**Cowboy Cookie Mix:**

Empty jar into a large mixing bowl; blend mix together. Add:

1 stick butter, melted                    1 egg, slightly beaten
1 teaspoon vanilla

Mix until thoroughly blended. Shape generous teaspoon-sized balls 2 inches apart on greased cookie sheet. Bake at 350 degrees for 11–13 minutes until edges are lightly browned. Cool 5 minutes on baking sheet, then remove cookies to racks to finish cooling.

# Molasses Cookie Mix

*These old-fashioned chewy, spicy cookies are delightful.*

Layer in a 1-quart jar:

2 cups flour
1 teaspoon baking soda
1 teaspoon cinnamon
$\frac{1}{4}$ teaspoon cloves
1 teaspoon ginger

1 cup sugar
1 teaspoon baking powder
$\frac{1}{2}$ teaspoon nutmeg
$\frac{1}{8}$ teaspoon allspice

Attach recipe that follows to jar:

**Molasses Cookies:**

Preheat oven to 375 degrees. In large bowl, mix:

¾ cup butter or margarine, softened     1 egg
¼ cup sulfured molasses

Add the cookie mix; beat until smooth. Shape the dough into 1-inch balls. Roll in granulated sugar. Place 2 inches apart on ungreased cookie sheets. Bake for 9–11 minutes. Cool on wire racks.

# Sand Art Brownies

*A fun gift to put together!*

Layer in 1-quart jar:

½ cup plus 2 teaspoons flour

⅓ cup cocoa

⅔ cup brown sugar

½ cup semisweet chocolate chips

½ cup walnuts and pecan pieces

⅔ teaspoon salt

½ cup flour

⅔ cup sugar

½ cup vanilla baking chips

Attach recipe that follows to jar:

**Sand Art Brownies:**

Add:

1 teaspoon vanilla           ⅓ cup oil
1 egg                        ⅓ cup warm water

Bake at 350 degrees:

9x9-inch pan 27–33 minutes
7x11-inch pan 32–37 minutes

# A Christmas Cookie Blessing

*May your cookie jar always be half full—*

*Because you've shared some with your family.*

*May you have good friends*

*with whom to share most of the rest.*

*But in the middle of the night*

*When you cannot sleep,*

*May there always be two left*

*For when you chat with the Almighty.*